SPOTLIGHT ON EXPLORERS AND COLONIZATION™

# FRANCISCO PIZARRO

## Conqueror of the Inca Empire

DANIEL TOLEDO

**ROSEN** PUBLISHING®

New York

Published in 2017 by The Rosen Publishing Group, Inc.
29 East 21st Street, New York, NY 10010

First Edition

**Library of Congress Cataloging-in-Publication Data**

Names: Toledo, Daniel (Daniel J.), author.
Title: Francisco Pizarro : conqueror of the Inca Empire / Daniel Toledo.
Description: First edition. | New York : Rosen Publishing, 2017. | Series:
  Spotlight on explorers and colonization | Includes bibliographical
  references and index. | Audience: Grade 7 to 12.
Identifiers: LCCN 2016000175| ISBN 9781477788042 (library bound) | ISBN
  9781477788028 (pbk.) | ISBN 9781477788035 (6-pack)
Subjects: LCSH: Pizarro, Francisco, approximately 1475–1541. |
  Peru—History—Conquest, 1522–1548. | Conquerors—Peru—Biography. |
  Conquerors—Spain—Biography. | Explorers—Peru—Biography. |
  Explorers—Spain—Biography.
Classification: LCC F3442.P776 T65 2016 | DDC 985/.02092—dc23
LC record available at http://lccn.loc.gov/2016000175

*Manufactured in the United States of America*

# CONTENTS

# BIRTH AND EARLY YEARS

Francisco Pizarro was a Spanish conquistador who settled the capital city of Lima, Peru. He journeyed across the Atlantic Ocean, through South America, and was responsible for subduing the Inca Empire. Pizarro was born in Trujillo, Spain, most likely between 1475 and 1478. His mother, whose name may have been Francisca González, came from a poor background. Francisco's father, Gonzalo Pizarro, was an infantry captain. Through his father, Francisco was related to Hernán Cortés. Cortés would later find his own fame as a conquistador. The distant cousins never met.

Pizarro came from humble beginnings. He was born out of wedlock, and could not inherit property. He could not read or write, and he had no prospects. Because of this, Pizarro became a swine handler. Later on, he joined the military, but failed to rise in rank like his father. Still, he wanted more from life. There was only one option for men of his background. And so in 1502, already in his thirties, Francisco Pizarro set sail for Hispaniola, the island that was the Spanish base in the New World.

# A FAILED SETTLEMENT

In 1508, Pizarro joined an expedition to the northern edge of South America. Alonso de Ojeda led the expedition. Ojeda had traveled with Christopher Columbus on Columbus's second journey to Hispaniola. Alonso de Ojeda's expedition landed in unexplored territory. They traveled along the coast of what is today Venezuela and Colombia. They even set up the colony of San Sebastián on the eastern side of the Gulf of Urabá.

The Spaniards had a difficult time in San Sebastián. The native tribes were hostile to the Spanish intruders. They waited outside the colony's walls with poisoned arrows. In addition to the native threat, the settlers

Alonso de Ojeda speaks to Native Americans from South America in this drawing. Ojeda's men were sick and dying. They did not get help from the local tribes.

suffered from tropical diseases and starvation. Out of the 300 people who set sail on the expedition, 200 died. While waiting for reinforcements from Hispaniola, Ojeda abandoned San Sebastián, leaving Pizarro in charge. Ojeda never returned.

The explorer Martín Fernández de Enciso finally arrived with supplies. On his ship was a stowaway named Vasco Núñez de Balboa. Balboa would play a large part in Pizarro's future success. The Spanish abandoned San Sebastián and set up a new colony across the Gulf of Urabá.

# THE SOUTH SEA

The Spanish named their new settlement Santa María la Antigua del Darién (the eastern part of the Isthmus of Panama was, and is, known as Darién). In Santa María, Pizarro teamed up with Vasco Núñez de Balboa. Balboa had once owned property in Hispaniola, but fell into debt. He escaped his creditors by fleeing. His luck was on the rise, though. After the settlers of Darién revolted against Martin Fernández de Enciso, Balboa was chosen as the new leader.

While Balboa and his men treated many of the natives badly, they tried to charm others with gifts. It was from a native leader that

In 1513 Vasco Núñez de Balboa became the first European to see the Pacific Ocean from the New World. This illustration shows Balboa and his men seeing the "South Sea" from a cliff for the first time.

Balboa heard that a great body of water lay to the south. In 1513, Pizarro and 189 others joined Balboa's expedition to find it. They marched across the Isthmus of Panama and found the Pacific Ocean. Balboa claimed it in the name of Spain. He called it the *Mar del Sur*, which means "South Sea." This discovery suggested that an ocean lay between the New World and Asia. It was an important moment for the explorers.

# NEW PARTNERS

After the expedition to the Pacific, Pizarro and Balboa gained wealth and recognition. However, despite Balboa's success, he failed to keep rising in rank. An aristocrat with ties to the crown, Pedro Arias Dávila, was appointed to take his place as the governor of Darién. Seeing the change of power, Pizarro conspired with Dávila against Balboa. Under Dávila's orders, Pizarro arrested his former friend and colleague. Dávila had Balboa executed in 1519.

Pizarro's loyalty to Dávila made him rich. From 1519 to 1523, he even served as the mayor of the town of Panamá, which had recently been founded. But Pizarro was still

This sixteenth-century engraving shows Pizarro, Almagro, and Luque (all seated) planning their expedition to Peru.

ambitious. He had heard rumors of gold in South America. Pizarro found two partners to help him pursue these riches. They were Diego de Almagro, a Spaniard who was also from humble beginnings, and Hernando de Luque, a Catholic priest. Together, the trio planned their conquest. Pizarro appointed himself expedition leader. Almagro was in charge of preparing the ships, while Luque would stay behind to maintain a good relationship with the governor.

# PIZARRO'S FIRST VOYAGE

In 1524, Pizarro set out on a reconnaissance mission down south, while Almagro recruited more men. Almagro was to join Pizarro after securing a second small ship. The company of eighty men struggled to survive in the new territory. Their food supplies ran low. They ate what fruit they could find to survive.

Hunger was just one of the challenges that the group faced. The Spaniards fought with many of the native people they encountered. Sickness and battle killed many of Pizarro's men. The terrain made the journey more difficult. The survivors struggled to get through the coastal swamps

plagued with insects. In the meantime, Almagro attempted to rejoin Pizarro, but was unable to find him. Less than a year after leaving, everyone returned to Panama without ever having made it farther south than the San Juan River in Colombia.

Pizarro's first mission was a failure, but he would not give up. He knew there were great riches in the south. The partners prepared for a second expedition.

# A SECOND EXPEDITION

Pizarro's second voyage took place from 1526 to 1528. This time 160 men volunteered for the expedition. Unlike before, Pizarro and his men were prepared this time around. Their two ships were full of horses, food, wine, and weapons. Pizarro and Almagro split up once they reached the San Juan River. Almagro returned to Panama with samples of gold to encourage more men to join the expedition. Pizarro remained with a group of men to explore inland.

As Pizarro explored the swamps along the coast, he told the expedition's pilot, Bartolomé Ruiz, to sail farther south. Ruiz would be responsible for finding out what

A Spanish conquistador from Pizarro's time would have worn armor like this. He would also have been accompanied by a foot soldier ready with a gun.

was beyond the Equator. He returned with news that the rumored rich lands did exist. Ruiz had encountered an Inca trading craft carrying silver, gold, gems, and fine cloth. He enslaved three of the Incas as language interpreters. Language interpreters were important to the Spaniards. Meanwhile Pizarro, camped on an island off the coast of what is now Colombia, was facing a mutiny in his camp.

# THE LINE IN THE SAND

**W**hile Almagro gathered recruits, Pizarro tried to keep his men in line. The men were disillusioned after not finding the promised riches. Pizarro knew he had to inspire them to push forward. According to legend, Pizarro drew a line in the sand with the tip of his sword. He said on one side was "death, hardship, hunger, nakedness, and abandonment." Those who remained on that side should "return to Panama—to be poor!" Those who stepped over to Pizarro's side would continue the journey to Peru. Pizarro spoke the words, "You choose what best becomes you as brave Spaniards." It was a dare. Only thirteen of his men crossed to Pizarro's side.

Pizarro's small company kept traveling past what is now Ecuador. The men discovered the city of Tumbes, a distant outpost of the Inca Empire. Unlike at other locations, the Spaniards were welcomed there. Pizarro saw temples full of silver and gold. The natives even had plates made of gold and gems on their clothes. It was the proof Pizarro needed. He returned to Spain to get royal permission to conquer Peru.

This woodcut shows the famous moment when Pizarro drew his line in the sand. Only thirteen men would follow him to Ecuador.

# RETURN TO SPAIN

**W**hen Pizarro returned to Spain, he had been gone for two decades. He was there to make the argument that he should lead the conquest of the Inca Empire in Peru. Governor Dávila wanted to lead his own expedition into Nicaragua. He refused to aid Pizarro. Upon his return to Spain, Pizarro presented the king—who was also the Holy Roman Emperor Charles V—with the riches of South America. The king was eager for more gold. He granted Pizarro ships, soldiers, and spies. Pizarro was now equipped to take on the Inca Empire. Pizarro recruited four of his half brothers

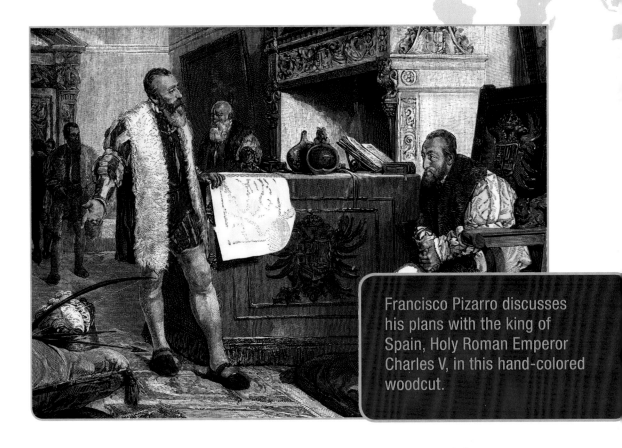

Francisco Pizarro discusses his plans with the king of Spain, Holy Roman Emperor Charles V, in this hand-colored woodcut.

and other men from his native town with promises of wealth.

Pizarro's license, or *capitulación*, gave him commanding power over his expedition and all conquered lands. Pizarro was also given the title of governor and captain general of Peru. This success caused friction with Almagro. Almagro didn't believe he was getting fair share of the glory. The tension between the two men would eventually lead to their deaths.

# THE INCA EMPIRE

The Inca who Pizarro hoped to conquer were a complex civilization. Their empire spread from Ecuador throughout Peru, Bolivia, and parts of Chile. The legends of the Inca claimed that their first leader, Manco Capac, was born from the sun. Their history was steeped in myth and legend. They lived in the valleys of the Andes Mountains. Cuzco was the city at the center of the Inca Empire.

Huayna Capac was the Sapa Inca, or Inca emperor, until 1527. He died suddenly from smallpox, which had been introduced into the New World by the Spanish. Huayna Capac's death led to division in the Inca Empire. Two of his sons, Huáscar and

This is Saksaywaman, a citadel on the outskirts of Cuzco, Peru. The stone structure is typical of Inca engineering.

Atahualpa, each claimed the throne. They launched a civil war that killed thousands of Incas. Atahualpa emerged as the victor, keeping Huáscar as prisoner. Huáscar still had loyal followers, though. This rift in the empire would help Pizarro conquer the Incas. Atahualpa's reign over the Inca Empire would be short.

# THE CONQUEST BEGINS

**P**izarro and his brothers started to travel for Peru in 1531. Their Inca-born translator, Felipillo, accompanied them. They had three ships and more than 200 men. The expedition sailed to Tumbes to pick up where Pizarro had last left off. Almagro and Luque remained behind, as usual, to raise money and reinforcements. The journey was so rough by boat that they chose to travel over land part of the way. However, the journey on foot proved just as challenging.

When the Spanish arrived at Tumbes, they found a city that had been torn apart by the Inca civil war. In Tumbes Pizarro and

his men were joined by reinforcements led by Hernando de Soto, who had traveled south from what is now Nicaragua. De Soto brought over a hundred men, horses, and supplies with him. Pizarro set up camp in what was later called San Miguel. Pizarro knew he was on the right path. He marched on inland, where would use the civil war to his advantage.

# STRATEGIC ALLIANCES

Soon after leaving San Miguel, the Spanish headed into the Andes Mountains. The ground was steep and the weather was cold. The roads the Spaniards found were ill suited to their horses and carts. They had been built for people traveling on foot or trains of sure-footed llamas.

As he pressed on toward the center of the Inca Empire, Pizarro made alliances with natives who were still loyal to the defeated and imprisoned Huáscar. Locals told Pizarro that Atahualpa was camped out in the city of Cajamarca. As the Spaniards journeyed through the Andes, representatives from Atahualpa's court met them on the road. The Inca ambassadors gave the Spaniards gold,

This illustration shows Francisco Pizarro leading his men through the steep roads of the Andes. He is on the way to his fateful meeting with the Inca ruler, Atahualpa, in Cajamarca.

wool, llamas, and other goods. Despite this hospitality, the Spanish treated the Incas with violence and brutality.

Atahualpa agreed to meet Pizarro in Cajamarca. It is unclear why Atahualpa would agree to this meeting. He was likely focused on the turmoil within the Inca Empire and didn't believe the Spaniards were a threat. He had just defeated his own brother and was now the thirteenth ruler of the Incas.

# ATAHUALPA'S CAPTURE

Pizarro sent a small group of men to meet with Atahualpa outside Cajamarca. Though some accounts suggest that the Spaniards unwittingly insulted the Inca leader during the meeting, Atahualpa nevertheless invited the Spanish force to spend the night in one of the royal buildings on Cajamarca's town square. He said he would meet Pizarro and his forces in the town the following day. At this point, Atahualpa didn't fear the Spanish and their small army.

When Atahualpa and his men arrived to meet the Spanish, Pizarro sent out a priest, Vicente de Valverde, to convert them to Christianity. The proud Atahualpa refused

conversion, throwing down a Bible that the priest showed him. At that point, Pizarro ordered his men to attack.

The Spanish had been hiding all around the square. They sprang out with their guns and slaughtered many Inca. The Inca had come prepared for a diplomatic meeting, not a battle. Despite their small numbers, the Spanish massacred thousands of Inca. Atahualpa was taken prisoner.

# RANSOM AND BETRAYAL

Atahualpa tried to secure his freedom by ransoming himself with silver and gold. Pizarro promised to free the Inca leader, as long as he got the agreed-upon ransom— enough to fill a room once with gold and twice with silver. Precious objects were gathered from every corner of the empire to make up the ransom. Atahualpa asked Pizarro to keep the items intact. But the Spaniard broke his promise and, in the end, melted the objects down to make the gold and silver easier to transport. Charles V was shipped his fifth of the loot. Pizarro kept a large portion of the rest, and the remainder was split among the other Spaniards.

After the ransom had been paid, the Spanish betrayed Atahualpa. When the news arrived that Huáscar had been killed, Pizarro accused Atahualpa of being involved and also of plotting against the Spanish. He had the Inca leader tried, sentenced to death, and executed. According to some accounts Atahualpa converted to Christianity before he died and was therefore granted a more dignified death.

# MARCH FOR CUZCO

**E**mboldened by Pizarro's victory over Atahualpa, the Spanish marched on to the Inca capital, Cuzco, in 1533. By this point things had changed between the original partners, Almagro, Luque, and Pizarro. Luque was dead and Almagro felt that he was being cheated out of his share of the Inca treasure. Pizarro had grown greedy and didn't want to share. He told Almagro they would split the riches they found in Cuzco. But when they reached Cuzco, the former partners couldn't agree on who was in control. In 1535, Almagro left for Chile to seek his own fortune.

In the meantime Pizarro realized that, with Huáscar and Atahualpa dead, he needed a

Francisco Pizarro was not as young as other conquistadors when he started his expeditions. Here, Pizarro is illustrated as an older man, having defeated the Inca Empire despite his age.

way to control the native population. He named one of their brothers as the new leader of Incas. The plan was for him to be a puppet leader, while the Spanish held the real power. When the leader who Pizarro had picked died, he placed yet another brother, Manco Inca, on the throne.

# THE PRICE OF GOLD

The Spanish spread out to conquer more of South America. While his brother Hernando stayed in Cuzco to keep control of it for the Spanish, Francisco Pizarro set off towards the seacoast. He founded a new capital, Lima, there in 1535. He called the town the "City of Kings."

Meanwhile, the Spanish continued to establish their control over the Incas. Most of the Inca royal family was killed. Inca women were forced to marry conquistadors. Pizarro himself married an Inca woman who became known as Inés Yupangui.

The Incas suffered torture at the hands of soldiers. They were forced to pay taxes to their Spanish rulers. Disease caused deaths on both sides. During this time, Manco Inca

secretly plotted a revolt. He was tired of the way the Spanish treated his people. In 1536, he led a rebellion against the Spanish. The Incas won several battles against the Spanish and laid siege to Cuzco for several months. In 1537, Almagro and his men returned from Chile and drove off Manco's forces. Some accounts say that before Almagro attacked, he tried unsuccessfully to form an alliance with Manco against Pizarro.

# THE SPANISH RIFT

**A**lmagro's expedition to Chile had been unsuccessful. He still hadn't received his share of Atahualpa's ransom. He felt marginalized by Pizarro and his brothers. Charles V told Pizarro and Almagro they could each rule over the lands they had conquered. However both conquistadors claimed the right to govern Cuzco. Now rivals for the same territory, Pizarro and Almagro began to fight. After ending the siege of Cuzco, Almagro seized power in the city and threw two of Pizarro's brothers into jail.

As the fighting continued, Almagro was emerging as victor. He defeated a force led by Pizarro's lieutenant, Pedro de Alvarado.

This illustration of Diego de Almagro with a sword and shield dates from the sixteenth centuty. Almagro had been Pizarro's partner in conquest, but was killed by the man he once trusted.

The fighting stopped for a while but soon resumed. It was Hernando Pizarro who eventually captured Almagro. He was held as prisoner and then killed. Hernando didn't stop there. He displayed Almagro's body for all to see. Pizarro and his brothers were victors. However, the enemies of the Pizarro family were fueled with anger. This would lead to their downfall.

# PIZARRO'S END

Pizarro had come a long way from the young swine handler he was in Spain. He had discovered new lands and found riches for the Spanish crown. Almagro was dead, which left him to claim Cuzco. After several failed attempts, Manco Inca had given up trying to reclaim Cuzco and set up a base in the mountainous and forested Vilcabamba Valley. Pizarro was in a great place to lead. The Spanish wanted more gold. They enslaved native peoples in silver and gold mines. Pizarro built himself a palace in Lima. At 66, Pizarro would not have time to enjoy the wealth he gained.

Almagro had a son who was also named Diego de Almagro. The son's nickname was

Despite his riches and conquest, Pizarro met a gruesome death in his palace in Lima, Peru. He was killed by Almagro's son and followers.

El Mozo. El Mozo wanted revenge for his father's death. He conspired with those still loyal to Almagro. El Mozo and his followers broke into Pizarro's palace. Pizarro attempted to fight for his life, but was wounded. It is said that Pizarro drew a cross on the floor out of his blood. Then he said a prayer and died on June 26, 1541.

# THE FIGHTING CONTINUES

**E**l Mozo's followers declared him the governor of Peru. However, he would not stay in power for long. After hearing about the fighting between Almagro's followers and Pizarro's, Charles V sent Cristóbal Vaca de Castro to take control of Peru. Vaca de Castro teamed up with the remaining Pizarro supporters to defeat those loyal to Almagro, called the "Almagristas," at the Battle of Chupas, on September 16, 1542. Soon after the battle El Mozo was captured and executed.

After their defeat, a handful of Almagristas fled to Manco Inca, asking for his protection. However the Almagristas soon decided to betray Manco in the hopes of winning back the favor of Peru's Spanish leaders. They murdered their host and tried to flee to Cuzco, but were killed by Incas avenging Manco's death.

Though their enemies had been defeated, things were not looking good for the Pizarro family. They lost much of their wealth after Francisco's murder. Hernando Pizarro was imprisoned in Spain for Almagro's death. Their brother Gonzalo tried to keep the family in power by fighting against the viceroys installed by Charles V. He was unsuccessful, though, and was executed in 1548.

# PIZARRO'S LEGACY

**W**hile some Incas continued to fight against the Spanish, they had little real success after Manco Inca's death. In time, most Incas assimilated to Spanish culture. They began to dress like Spaniards and convert to Christianity. Temples were pillaged and destroyed. As more Spanish people came to settle Peru, the Inca way of life was lost. The Inca culture was replaced by the Spanish way of life. Though some Inca descendants still live in the Andes, they are a small group.

Pizarro's conquest of the Inca Empire had been brutal. His methods were cruel, and many people died. Pizarro's desire for wealth and power led to his death. Like other

Though Peru is now a modern country, the Inca ways live on in some areas. These women in traditional clothing are in Chivay, Peru.

conquistadors, he is now often seen in a negative light. His violence brought down a whole civilization.

However, it was also a major military victory, one that many people had thought impossible. Pizarro had few soldiers, but still managed to conquer a large, powerful empire. His actions shaped what Peru is today. Pizarro's tomb is still in Lima, Peru, the city he founded in 1535.

# GLOSSARY

**alliances** Agreements to work together toward a goal.

**assimilated** Took on the lifestyle of another culture.

*capitulación* A license from the king of Spain to conquer a place.

**conquistador** One of the Spanish explorers who conquered parts of Central and South America in the sixteenth century.

**convert** To get people to change their religion.

**colony** An area that is under the control of a foreign country and inhabited by people from that country.

**Equator** The imaginary line that divides earth into a northern half and a southern half.

**equipped** Supplied with what is needed for a task.

**expedition** A journey taken by a group with the aim of exploration, research, or war.

**infantry** The part of a military that fights on foot.

**isthmus** A narrow piece of land that separates two larger pieces of land.

**New World** The name the Europeans gave to the Americas during the Age of Discovery.

**prospects** Potential to gain success or wealth.

**ransoming** Trading money for a person's freedom.

**reconnaissance** Gathering information about something, especially about an enemy in wartime.

**reinforcements** New people and supplies who arrive to help an existing force or group.

**viceroys** People sent by a king to rule a colony.

The Gilder Lehrman Institute of American History
49 West 45th Street, 6th Floor
New York, NY 10036
(646) 366-9666
Website: http://www.gilderlehrman.org/history
  -now/2007-06/age-exploration
The Gilder Lehrman Institute of American History
  was founded to promote and support history
  education. The group's comprehensive website has
  information on the Age of Exploration with links for
  teachers.

Institute of Andean Studies
PO Box 9307
Berkeley, CA 94709
Website: http://www.instituteofandeanstudies.org
The Institute of Andean Studies conducts research
  and study on the former Inca Empire. It has a
  journal dedicated to the past and holds an annual
  meeting.

Latin American Institute at UCLA
10343 Bunche Hall
Los Angeles, CA 90095
(310) 825-4571
Website: http://www.international.ucla.edu/lai/
  article/104063

Founded in 1959, the Latin American Institute has resources and workshops dedicated to Latin American studies. The institute also puts out several publications and is involved in teacher training.

Spanish Studies Institute at UNL
61B Henzlik Hall
Lincoln, NE 68588
(402) 472-0683
Website: http://cehs.unl.edu/tlte/spanish-studies -institute/
Spanish Studies Institute supports the teaching of Spanish language and Hispanic cultures. It runs summer courses for students and teachers, as well as a program for teachers from Spain to visit the United States.

# Websites

Because of the changing nature of Internet links, Rosen Publishing has developed an online list of websites related to the subject of this book. This site is updated regularly. Please use this link to access the list:

http://www.rosenlinks.com/SEC/pizar

*Aztec, Inca & Maya (DK Eyewitness Books)*. New York, NY: DK Publishing, 2011.

Dalrymple, Lisa, and Cynthia O'Brien. *Explore with Francisco Pizarro (Travel with the Great Explorers)*. New York, NY: Crabtree Publishing, 2015.

DiConsiglio, John. *Francisco Pizarro: Destroyer of the Inca Empire (Wicked History)*. New York, NY: Franklin Watts, 2009.

Lewin, Ted. *Lost City: The Discovery of Machu Picchu*. New York, NY: Philomel, 2003.

Newman, Sandra. *The Inca Empire*. New York, NY: Children's Press, 2010.

Sonneborn, Liz. *Pizarro: Conqueror of the Mighty Incas.* Berkeley Heights, NJ: Enslow, 2010.

Waldron, Melanie. *Geography Matters in the Inca Empire*. North Mankato, MN: Heinemann-Raintree, 2015.

Zronik, John Paul. *Francisco Pizarro: Journeys Through Peru and South America*. New York: Crabtree Publishing, 2005.

Zronik, John Paul. *Hernando Cortés: Spanish Invader of Mexico*. New York, NY: Crabtree Publishing, 2007.

# BIBLIOGRAPHY

Celerier, Luis R. "San Sebastian & Nombre de Dios" Bits & Pieces—History of Panama. April 5, 2011 (http://www.panamahistorybits.com/article.asp?id=2011-04-05).

"Francisco Pizarro." The Mariners' Museum: The Ages of Exploration. Retrieved January 29, 2016 (http://exploration.marinersmuseum.org/subject/francisco-pizarro/).

Gabai, Rafael Varón. *Francisco Pizarro and His Brothers: Illusion of Power in Sixteenth-Century Peru*. Translated by Javier Flores Espinoza. Norman, OK: University of Oklahoma Press, 1997.

"Huayna Capac." Maya, Inca, Aztec. Retrieved January 29, 2016 (http://mayaincaaztec.com/huaynacapac.html).

Lobell, Jarrett A., and Eric A. Powell. "In Search of History's Greatest Rulers." *Archaeology*. July 16, 2013 (http://archaeology.org).

MacQuarrie, Kim. *The Last Days of the Incas*. New York, NY: Simon & Schuster, 2007.

Seaman, Rebecca M., Ed. *Conflict in the Early Americas: An Encyclopedia of the Spanish Empire's Aztec, Incan, and Mayan Conquests*. Santa Barbara, CA: ABC-CLIO, 2013.

Wood, Michael. *Conquistadors*. Berkeley, CA: University of California Press, 2001.

# INDEX

# About the Author

Daniel Toledo was born in Guayaquil, Ecuador, studied English Literature and Latino Studies at the University of Montana, and lives in New York City.

# Photo Credits